FRANCISCO GOYA

FRANCISCO GOYA

Claus Virch

Department of European Paintings

Metropolitan Museum of Art

McGRAW-HILL BOOK COMPANY   NEW YORK · LONDON · TORONTO · SYDNEY

Cover picture, *Three Men Digging* (about 1819), sepia wash drawing, Metropolitan Museum of Art, New York, Harris Brisbane Dick Fund, 1935.

GOYA, as is now generally agreed, ranks with the greatest painters of our Western culture. The story of his life, especially its legendary aspects, has excited the public imagination because it appeals to our conception of the artist as a romantic, if not tragic figure. He has been hailed as a modern painter, as a forerunner of the Expressionists. His general recognition and worldwide fame, however, are of a rather recent date. In the nineteenth century, only a few men, among them the French painters Delacroix, Daumier and Manet, and the writer Théóphile Gautier, grasped his importance. It is often the case that artists are the first to re-discover the achievements of the past.

Except for a few etchings, hardly anything could be seen of the works of the great Goya outside of Spain, and even those who undertook the arduous journey found little. In Goya's own day, his portraits hung in royal apartments or private collections that could be entered only with the proper introductions. Many of the extraordinary works on which his fame is now chiefly based could not be seen at all: the many wonderful drawings, the rolled-up and long-forgotten cartoons for tapestries, the powerful Black Paintings on the walls of his country house, or the etchings of the *Caprichos* series (of which only a few copies were sold before the printing was stopped), not to mention *Los Desastres de la Guerra (The Disasters of War)* or other graphic productions that were never published during Goya's lifetime. This situation has changed completely as more and more books and exhibitions have exposed every aspect of Goya's work. Acclaimed in his own time as an artist of surprising talent, he is now recognized as a man of genius whose exceptional gifts are better understood every day. As we search deeper into man's soul, as we experience wars more cruel than ever, as new movements and inventions open our eyes to the ever-changing character of art, we understand more fully how prophetic, profound and daringly modern Goya was.

Most visitors to the Prado in Madrid now head for Goya's paintings rather than for those by Velázquez, who is equally well represented in this great museum. Goya is said to have claimed Velázquez, Rembrandt and Nature as his masters. He learned a great deal from Velázquez whose paintings he copied in early, curiously awkward etchings, whose royal portraits formed prototypes for his own, and whose brilliant, fluid brushwork and treatment of flat areas in subtly shaded earth colors are found in much of Goya's early work. In temperament, however, he was totally different from Velázquez, who remained always a detached and uninvolved observer. Many more analogies can be found between Goya and the northern titan, Rembrandt. Both artists began splendidly as fashionable portrait painters of the upper classes, and revelled in early social and monetary success, after which they withdrew more and more into their own worlds, creating their works from imagination and observation without concession to contemporary taste. Both were rather uneducated men of humble

Frontispiece.
Self Portrait
(about 1795)
wash drawing in India ink
6″ x 3⁹⁄₁₆″
Metropolitan Museum of Art
New York
Harris Brisbane Dick Fund, 1935

[Facing this page]
Detail of Figure 5

5

origin, but they conquered their country's capitals and gained the friendship of scholars whose learning supported their intuitive artistic wisdom. Their subjects were rarely landscapes or still-lifes, their concern was man. Both were touchingly devoted to an only surviving son, Rembrandt to Titus, and Goya to Javier. Stretching the point still further, both men, in their lonely late years, were much attached to their housekeeper-companions, Rembrandt to Hendrickje Stoffels, the model of many of his most beautiful late pictures, and Goya to Leocadia Weiss, a woman of disputable qualities. As both artists sank into oblivion within their own lifetimes, they expressed their thoughts in innumerable drawings and etchings, and their graphic work spread the knowledge of their genius to a few connoisseurs in the far corners of Europe. Though far apart in time and place, the Dutchman and the Spaniard, each proudly aware of his calling, explored deeper and deeper regions of the human condition, one discovering the world of God, the other that of Satan.

Art history, fitting styles into centuries for convenience, has created its own terminology. Thus, the eighteenth century is characterized as the period of the easy, witty, frivolous and decorative rococo, the nineteenth century as an age of surging, emotional romanticism and a new, realistic look at man and nature. Goya began as the darling of a Francophile society, providing decorative tapestry designs and splendid portraits for its taste. Had he died young, before the close of the eighteenth century, he would perhaps hardly be remembered as more than a provincial cousin of Boucher and Fragonard. However, his career, equally divided between the centuries, was affected by the beginning of a new epoch that allowed the artist a wider range of vision and expression. Art was no longer a means in the pursuit of happiness. Goya learned a tragic sense of life, and depicts modern man, beset by anxieties and exposed to a greedy, restless world. In retrospect we discover an underlying skepticism and satire in his earlier work as well, hinting at the hollowness of the old order that was soon to break asunder. Goya's "message" was never the tiresome, academic beauty sought after and taught during his youth by the now forgotten pope of Spanish art, Anton Raphael Mengs, but rather the inescapable, cruel truth about the world around us as well as the world within. Idealization, stylization, flattery, all that "beautifies" and detracts from the truth, are totally absent from his mature works. That the expression of such truth was possible and permissible in the Spain of Goya's time is quite inexplicable. If the king did not detect the slanderous implications of the *Caprichos* etchings as we interpret them today, but instead gratefully accepted the plates as a present, we can imagine that the time-consuming sport of hunting prevented him from taking a look at them. Yet how could the less stupid, vain queen delight in seeing herself depicted as an overdressed wanton witch with a bulbous nose, and gladly endure arduous sittings for more such portraits?

In the nineteenth century Spain was newly discovered by the rest of Europe as a strange and alien, but highly picturesque country. Adventure books such as Washington Irving's *Tales of the Alhambra,* plays and operas like Bizet's *Carmen,* the opening to the public of the famous "Galerie Espagnol" in the Louvre in 1838, containing 412 Spanish paintings assembled by King Louis-Philippe (including several by Goya), and similar events helped to stimulate the exotic image of Spain as a nation of proud and fierce passions. Goya was

easily made into a romantic hero and quickly became a victim of the lore of Spain. Every anecdote, rumor, and scandal regarding his life was collected, exaggerated and repeated in the earliest literary accounts of the artist published in the nineteenth century which read like picaresque novels. Thanks to these early biographies, Goya still lives today as the bravado bullfighter, the dashing lady-killer, the extravagant courtier who amused with witty caricature sketches, the passionate lover of the Duchess of Alba, the hot-blooded patriot, and last, the lonely, deaf man who created visionary masterpieces in the solitude of his country house. Some modern books still perpetuate the old stories that seem too colorful and entertaining to be simply abandoned. At the same time, new facts brought to light by scholarly research iconoclastically destroy many romantic feats attributed to Goya. While the glorious legend of his life grows dimmer, the conditions under which his work was created become clearer.

Francisco José de Goya y Lucientes was born in Fuendetodos, a small village near Saragossa, capital of the former kingdom of Aragon. The extremely modest house at No. 18 Calle de Alfóndiga, in which he was born on March 30, 1746 still stands. His father, José Goya, was a gilder by profession, but at the time of the artist's birth, he humbly tilled a small piece of land which had been the dowry of Goya's mother, Gracia Lucientes, who was descended from Aragonese nobility. Little is known about Goya's childhood except for anecdotes of the kind usually attached to the youth of great artists, such as the story of the mighty patron who, wandering through the countryside, discovers the child drawing a pig or sheep with charcoal on a stone and immediately recognizes his talent. Young Goya went to school in Saragossa (Figure 1) and there, at the Escuela Pía, directed by Father Joaquín, his lifelong friendship with Martín Zapater began. Goya's letters to his old school friend in Saragossa are among the most important documents regarding the painter's life, telling of his hopes and frustrations, boasting of honors and complaining about his health. As a gilder, José Goya must have known most of the artists in Saragossa, and once Francisco's career was decided upon he was apprenticed in 1760, aged fourteen, to the best local painter,

José Luzán. Although an unimportant imitator of Italian baroque painting, Luzán was a popular teacher. The tedious hours of academic training spent sketching plaster casts after the antique or copying prints are echoed in the critical remark which Goya supposedly made later about some academic painters: "They confuse their young pupils by making them trace for years, with sharply pointed pencils, almond-shaped eyes, mouths like arches or hearts, noses resembling the figure seven upside down, oval heads. Ah, if they were but allowed to study nature. Nature is the only master of drawing."

For the restless and ambitious pupil the natural goal was Madrid, metropolis and seat of the glittering court, the only place where lucrative commissions and fame could be won. In 1763 Goya competed for a scholarship at the Royal Academy, but without success. Three years later he tried again but did not win a single vote. By that time, however, he had reached Madrid. Luzán had probably arranged a place for him in the studio of another former pupil, Francisco Bayeu. In 1770 we find Goya in Rome, in 1771 back in Spain. His moves from Saragossa to Madrid, to Rome, and back are a saga of brawls, knifings and rapes. The irascible young Spaniard with a ready sword and a keen eye for the fair sex apparently was constantly run out of town. In Rome, for example, after various escapades such as climbing to the top of the dome of St. Peter's, he attempted to abduct a nun from a convent, and only the intervention of the Spanish ambassador saved him from the death penalty.

Putting romance aside, we can easily picture the student Goya, very poor and no longer very young, eagerly pursuing his career. Once he had gained Madrid, where painting was completely Italianate, the desire to go to Rome, the homeland of many centuries of art, seems only obvious. Generations of artists had made the pilgrimage to the Eternal City. The rising interest in the art of ancient Greece and Rome made it a special center of attraction during the second half of the eighteenth century. Goya, however, never showed the slightest interest in classical art. No echo of classical antiquity, as it pervaded and often dominated the work of his contemporaries, is ever found in his paintings or etchings. His sole interest was the present and life in Rome which, at that time, was as artistic, international and exciting as pre-World War I Paris.

By the end of 1771, attracted by possible church commissions, Goya had returned to Saragossa, which he always considered his native city. His first project there was for the town's second cathedral, Nuestra Señora del Pilar. The imposing building, rising majestically on the banks of the river Ebro, with its many-colored, tiled domes reflecting in the water, was begun in 1681 to replace a small shrine, and was at last ready to receive its interior decoration. Goya submitted his sketches for the frescoes of a vaulted ceiling and was granted the commission by the church authorities. For the next decade he painted many religious themes and decorations for other churches as well, including eleven large murals, rarely seen and now much ruined, for the Charterhouse of Aula Dei near Saragossa. Since the Middle Ages the Church had been the major patron of the arts, and Goya sought recognition on the path that had earned bread for generations of artists before him. It was a dead-end road, however. The end of the eighteenth and the advent of the nineteenth century saw events and developments that brought the common man to the fore, and weakened the structure of the Church more than Luther and European Protestantism had done earlier. The Catholic Church lost its world-wide power and its patronage declined.

In Spain, religious belief and fervor are most deeply expressed in the well-known paintings of El Greco, Zurbarán and Murillo and perhaps even more ardently in the works of minor painters and sculptors of the seventeenth century. Spanish art, more than that of most European countries, confessed a mystic belief in God. Goya probably was as good a Catholic as most of his countrymen and an obedient son of the Church, but religious transcendency held no real truth for him; as an artist he was therefore incapable of representing it. Most of his religious painting is today forgotten or overlooked, because it carries so little conviction and only repeats hollow pictorial conventions. In these works, Goya followed traditional baroque schemes, and continued the established style in Spanish church decoration that had been introduced by Luca Giordano and perpetuated by another Italian, Corrado Giaquinto, and his Spanish pupil, Antonio González Velázquez, all of them painting undistinguished works. Therefore, one need not assume that his commissions in Aragon resulted from his having travelled abroad to study the art of fresco-painting, but rather to his continuance of familiar decorative modes.

So far our romantic hero, as he is presented to us in literature, had adhered faithfully to the established pattern; first, the academic training with a home-town teacher, then the student's usual educational trip to Italy, followed by provincial church patronage. In accordance with a custom dating back to medieval times and the old guild system, he insured security, respectability and continuance of commissions by marrying into an artistic dynasty, however minor and new. In 1773, he married Josefa Bayeu, sister of Francisco and Ramón Bayeu, natives of Saragossa and also Luzán's former pupils, who by then had steadily progressed in their uninspired artistic careers.

Josefa was a quiet, self-effacing woman of whom little is known. In his letters to Zapater, Goya always speaks of her with respect and affection. His likeness of her (Figure 2) is one of his most sensitive and sympathetic portraits. With golden-red hair, fine limbs and large, expressive eyes, she must have been quite lovely in her youth. She is often said to have been the long-suffering wife of a philandering husband to whom she bore twenty children. The less sensational truth is that Goya probably had five children. Whether twenty or five, only one survived: his beloved son Javier.

Francisco Bayeu was in charge of further decorations in the cathedral of El Pilar and dutifully allowed his brother-in-law a share in it. Goya had worked successfully with Bayeu on previous projects, but for the first time, in 1780, his independent spirit asserted itself and revealed him as the insolent individual he was. In the course of decorating the four small cupolas of the chapel devoted to Our Lady, a family feud broke out because Goya did not deign to coördinate his designs with those of his older relative. Insults flew back and forth between the two artists. In the end, the bewildered church authorities forbade Goya to do any further work in the cathedral.

Later squabbles and jealousies notwithstanding, Goya benefited greatly from his marital relationship. Bayeu had been appointed court painter in 1765. In 1774, put in charge of new

designs for tapestries, he called for his younger brother Ramón and his brother-in-law as assistants, and thus opened the doors to the capital, the seat of Goya's ambitions.

Eighteenth century Madrid was bustling with activity and excitement. It was an artificial city, a political creation, wholly unsuited geographically and climatically to be the capital, except for being situated in the exact center of the country. By decree of Philip II it had become the royal residence in 1560, but while other, more mercantile Spanish cities like Seville or Cadíz flourished, Madrid remained a collection of small houses, with unpaved roads in the midst of a barren and treeless landscape. Until the middle of the eighteenth century it was considered the dirtiest capital in Europe and was compared to an African village, when the great change came about which turned it into one of the world's most sophisticated cities.

Figure 4.
Anton Raphael Mengs
Johan Joachim Winckelmann
(about 1760)
oil on canvas, 25″ x 19⅜″
Metropolitan Museum of Art, New York
Harris Brisbane Dick Fund, 1948

Figure 3.
Charles III in Hunting Dress
(1780)
oil on canvas, 82⅝″ x 50″
Prado, Madrid

In 1700 the last Hapsburg king of Spain had willed his throne to the house of the French Bourbons. With the reign of Philip V, the seventeenth century, the greatest century of Spanish art, ended. Under Ferdinand VI official art, as directed by the court, became a mixture of French and Italian imports. The peace-loving Ferdinand, a connoisseur of music, prepared a beneficial climate for one of Spain's best kings, Charles III of Naples (Figure 3), who reigned from 1759 to 1788. After 25 years as ruler of the Two Sicilies, Charles came to Spain as a wise, old monarch. He introduced a sound economy, curbed the out-of-hand power of Church and Inquisition and, among other things, patronized the arts. In 1761 he summoned Anton Raphael Mengs (Figure 4) to Spain and made him the kind of cultural coördinator that Charles Lebrun had been under Louis XIV and Boucher under Louis XV, responsible for all decorative schemes and royal ventures into the arts. Austrian by birth and Roman by choice, Mengs was a misguided genius. Although an artist of enormous talent and intelligence, Mengs, influenced by the classical theorist Winckelmann, propagated a theoretical neo-classicism that only served to stifle his own painting. His call for a return to antiquity found little response in Spain. However, his admirable, courtly portraits, which count among his best works, influenced the style of the young Goya and the whole Spanish school of portraiture; but it is as director of the Royal Tapestry Factory that Mengs merits most credit.

The workshops were founded in 1721 by Philip V in imitation of the French Royal Gobelin Factory and, since they were situated outside the city gates of Santa Bárbara, were named after the saint. Following French taste and tradition, the tapestries were woven after paintings by seventeenth century Flemish artists such as Teniers, under the direction of skilled craftsmen from Antwerp. Some French and Italian designs were also executed. Production slowly declined until Charles III put Mengs in charge. The world-famous foreigner decided to make use of native talent. When the English Major Dalrymple visited Madrid, as described in his *Travels through Spain and Portugal in 1774* (published 1777), he could still write: "The town swarms with French and Italian manufacturers and shopkeepers. If one hears of an artist, one is sure to find him a foreigner, for the arts have made but little progress amongst the natives." In that year, 1774, Mengs returned from Rome after a long absence and called in a host of young Spanish artists for the designing of tapestry cartoons. Among them was Francisco Bayeu, who in turn called for Goya. This was a propitious moment.

The king was tired of copies after paintings by Raphael in the royal collections. For the decoration of the "comedor" or dining hall of the princes at the Palace of El Escorial, he ordered tapestries showing his favorite pastimes, hunting and fishing. Not without reason was he nicknamed "El Rey Cazador," the hunter king. Mythology and similarly foreign themes were dropped in favor of scenes from Spanish life. Goya's first attempts at tapestry designs were so undistinguished that scholars long considered them works of the brothers Bayeu and other artists, until recent documentary proof established his authorship. Indeed, they follow the stilted conventions for which Bayeu is known.

The second series was designed for the Palace of El Pardo and the subject, officially determined by the king, was "the costumes and diversions of the time." This commission marks a turning point in Goya's career. Its theme influenced him profoundly as it enabled him to draw on his own observations. With quick-eyed perception he painted the colorful and picturesque side of Madrid life, *The Picnic on the Banks of the Manzanares, The Fair of Madrid, The Crockery Vendor, Young Lovers Under the Sunshade, Men Flying Kites,* and other similar scenes, full of play and fresh colors. From 1775 until 1792 he made no less than sixty-three cartoons for tapestries, among them *The Manikin* (Slide 5) which was one of the last. These paintings, for they are actually painted in oil on canvas, constitute a large body of Goya's work. As Watteau's Fêtes Galantes are typically French, and Tiepolo's carnival scenes are Venetian, so are Goya's tapestry designs unmistakably Spanish. A strong feeling for all things national in tradition, costumes, pastimes and feasts, was welling up within the country that had been dominated for so long by foreign rule and influence, and this movement was encouraged by the understanding old king. Goya captured the mood superbly, with warm imagination and increasing technical virtuosity in his use of color and brush. His cartoons present a lively panorama of Spain in her eighteenth century heyday, at a time when, elsewhere in Europe, such representations of real life were hampered by the artificial and bloodless values of classicism.

About 1788 Goya painted his most enchanting small picture, the *Pradera di San Isidro* (Figure 5), in which light and atmosphere are rendered so truthfully that this painting is rightly hailed as anticipating Impressionism. Most authors claim that it was a study for a tapestry cartoon that never reached the weaver. It is difficult to believe that Goya thought a weaver could ever reproduce the brilliant light, and the multitude of small figures who have made the pilgrimage across the river from the city to celebrate the saint's day on the fifteenth of May. This little jewel, with its odd shape of about one by three feet, painted in silvery hues, is the apotheosis of eighteenth century Madrid. The imposing bulk of the new Bourbon palace to the left, and the domed neo-classical pantheon of San Francisco el Grande at the right, loom large in the city's skyline. In 1734 a fire had broken out and had totally destroyed the former royal residence. The new palace, built on the most grandiose lines, had to be decorated in terms of the glorification of the Spanish monarchy. At this late date of European absolutism, no one was left for such a task but the aging Giovanni Battista Tiepolo, whose style had become old-fashioned in his native Venice. Born in 1696, the famous painter came to Madrid in 1762, accompanied by his two sons, Giovanni Domenico and Lorenzo, and filled the vast ceilings of the Royal Palace with his usual buoyant array of Olympian gods and

Figure 5.
Pradera di San Isidro
(1788)
oil on canvas, 17¼" x 37"
Prado, Madrid

Figure 6.
Giovanni Battisa Tiepolo,
*The Apotheosis of the
Spanish Monarchy* (1764)
oil sketch for ceiling decoration
in the Royal Palace, Madrid
32⅛" x 26⅛"
Metropolitan Museum of Art
New York
Rogers Fund, 1937

mythological figures (Figure 6). His light-colored frescoes are carried out in the genial, daring rococo manner so disapproved of by Mengs, and it is said that Tiepolo's death in 1770 was hastened by the latter's jealous intrigues. Giovanni Domenico returned to Venice soon thereafter, and Lorenzo died in Madrid in 1776. The Tiepolos were the last ambassadors of the great Venetian school of painting to Spain, an artistic relationship that had begun with the almost exclusive patronage of Titian by her kings Charles V and Philip II. The example of the Tiepolos freed Goya's palette, suggesting the sparkling hues which he used in some of the cartoons and in his frescoes in San Antonio de la Florida. Also Giovanni Battista's two series of etchings, the *Vari Capricci* and the *Scherzi di Fantasia* must have been known to Goya, and stimulated the beginning of his own career as one of the greatest graphic artists of all times.

After some early experimental etchings of religious subjects, Italianate in style, he etched in 1778 a series of 16 copies after paintings by Velázquez in the royal collections, no doubt commissioned by the Real Calcografía (royal printing press). Though clumsy and inept, these etchings show the technical influence of Tiepolo, and testify to Goya's often quoted study of Velázquez. This commission gained him access to the works of other great masters hung in the royal palaces, which are today the glory of the Prado Museum.

Yet, copying masterpieces and designing for tapestries held no great honors and was badly paid. Again and again, Goya tried his hand at religious subjects as the highest form of art and, however poor the outcome, slowly succeeded towards the ultimate goal, which in an absolute monarchy meant royal favor. In 1780 he submitted to the Academy of San Fernando his "Christ on the Cross," a dull and spiritless work that shows calculated borrowings both from the Crucifixion by the royal favorite Mengs, painted for the palace of Aranjuez, and from Velázquez' lifesize Christ, now in the Prado. Both prototypes hardly inspire religious feelings. Goya's Christ, an academically correct, realistic study from the model, at least earned him election to the Academy (Figure 7).

Figure 7.
Christ on the Cross
(1780)
oil on canvas
100⅜" x 60¼"
Prado, Madrid

The building of the vast church of San Francisco el Grande, begun in 1761, was nearing completion, and thanks to the intervention of friends, Goya was granted the king's permission to paint one of the seven altarpieces. Aware of its potential, he labored arduously over this task, so foreign to the creative designer of tapestry cartoons, and produced a second-rate painting that pleased everyone. His subject was "The Miracle of St. Bernardino of Siena preaching in the Presence of King Alfonso V." The unveiling of the altar paintings, the high altar having been allotted to Francisco Bayeu, took place in the presence of the king and a crowd of Madrid society on December 8, 1784. Goya wrote about his success to his friend Zapater a few days later: "I have been lucky with my St. Bernardino, not only with the critics but with the public as well. The king himself praised the picture before the entire court and the members of the Academy." He felt full of hope, yet was to be disappointed once again. In 1779 he had been graciously received by the king, but his petition for a court appointment had been refused. As a result of the critical acclaim for his altarpiece he was appointed Deputy Director of Painting at the Academy, a post "of little use and not much honor," as he wrote Zapater. Through Bayeu's lukewarm recommendation Goya was at least made official painter to the tapestry factory with a fixed salary in 1786. Although he seems to have been aware of Goya's special gifts, the king must have harbored a personal grudge against the opportunistic artist. Only after his death and the accession of Charles IV to the throne in 1789, did the greatest Spanish painter of his time finally receive the coveted title of Court Painter, thus joining the ranks of some twenty other court painters whose names mean nothing now.

He received relatively few commissions from his royal employer, but two of them stand out: the portrait of the family of Charles IV, Goya's only large group portrait and a milestone in the history of royal portraiture (Figure 8), and his decorations for San Antonio de la Florida (Slide 12), a triumph of his genius. It is ironic that this fresco cycle is his only really successful religious painting, for it is more an outburst of pagan splendor than an expression of religious devotion. The mystical element of religion, so foreign to Goya's vision, is submerged in an exuberant beehive of real life and, in a reversal of the established order, the angels are squeezed into minor spaces below the circle of real people. In appreciation of this work, Goya finally was made First Painter to the King, in 1799, the highest honor available to an artist in Spain at the end of a splendid century, when the doom of the monarchy was not yet apparent to those present.

While Goya vainly strove for royal recognition and public commissions as a religious painter, his star rose brilliantly in Madrid society. He became the portraitist of everyone who was important. In 1783 he painted the most powerful man in Spain next to the king, the Prime Minister, Count Floridablanca, who, incidentally, seems to have thought that such honor required no payment. "Well, Goya, we shall see later," he supposedly said, and in retrospect he was quite right, because display of the pompous, over-elaborate work immediately resulted in a flood of exalted commissions. Snob that he was, Goya proudly reported to Zapater all the honors he had received. The same year, the king's brother, Don Luis de Bourbon, invited him to his country seat to paint his family. Goya made friends with the

family, went hunting with the prince and was showered with gifts. His next order was for a series of portraits of officials of the Bank of San Carlos: these turned out as dull and conventional as portraits of such men usually do. Goya however, was "most contented and the happiest man in the world." He earned a lot of money—in fact, he was financially independent for the rest of his life—and cut off his allowances to poor relatives because he needed the money to maintain his newly elevated standard of living. He bought a fancy carriage out of which he promptly fell, spraining his ankle, and learned French to "parler" with his new chic friends and patrons.

This short period of late and exuberantly enjoyed success was soon sadly ended. In 1792 and 1793 Goya suffered the fateful illness that was to leave him totally and permanently deaf. Matheron, his most romantic biographer, completely suppresses any mention of the illness. Later writers quote Goya's son in relating an imaginary tale: the amorous artist was accompanying the young Duchess of Alba, banished to her country estates by the jealous

Figure 8.
The Family of Charles IV
(1800)
oil on canvas
110¼" x 132¼"
Prado, Madrid

queen for her liaison with a dashing bullfighter, when their coach collapsed in a lonely spot. Mending the coach by the heat of a fire, Goya subsequently caught a chill that led to his tragic illness. The truth is more complicated and still uncertain. While in Cadíz on a journey to the South, he was struck with a nervous disorder which temporarily paralyzed his hands and destroyed his hearing. He passed his convalescence in the house of Don Sébastian Martínez (Slide 6), and was able to paint actively again after his return to Madrid in 1793. The illness that suddenly attacked Goya, not syphilis as is often alleged but a strange syndrome medically termed Vogt-Koyanagi, is generally considered responsible for the gradual deepening of characterization in his work and for its increasingly bitter and satirical aspects. His days in search of happiness and success were over; life's true sense began to reveal itself through suffering as mad and sordid.

The series of splendid portraits continued, leaving us a complete gallery of the men and women of Goya's time: kings, princes, courtiers, politicians, scholars, writers, artists, bullfighters, ladies of rank, fashion and beauty, with most of whom he was also well acquainted, and children whom he painted lovingly. These portraits, spanning a period of almost forty-five years, record the changes of time, fashions and ideas. While Martínez is still the perfect representative of the eighteenth century, the enlightened gentleman safely ensconced in the old order, painted in delicate rococo hues (Slide 6), Satué is the man of the new century, the revolutionary, the liberal, informally posed, dressed in somber black, the predominant color of Goya's last phase, which he handles with vigorous freedom (Slide 19).

During Goya's lifetime, the wheel of history was turning doubly fast all over Europe. Taken as a group, his portraits fully illustrate this important, dramatic and turbulent chapter of Spain's past. Floridablanca's conservative efforts to stem the swelling tide in the face of the French Revolution were fruitless in the end. Goya's portrait (Figure 8) shows the royal family together for the last time. Missing in the portrait is the queen's favorite, Manuel de Godoy, then prime minister and over-honored "Prince of the Peace." Godoy was a cad of the first order, made more immortal by Goya's brush than by his own political misdeeds. The disintegration of the royal family followed soon afterwards in scenes worthy of comic opera, but resulted in years of miserable suffering for the people of Spain.

In October 1807 the king arrested his son Ferdinand for treasonable attempts to dethrone him and to murder the queen, his mother, as well as her lover Godoy. Whether or not the charge was true, Ferdinand was pardoned, but embarrassing statements, made public in the papers, clearly demonstrated the weakness of the government. Thus, encouraged by the situation, Napoleon sent his troops to Spain under shady pretexts. The Spanish, blaming the despised Godoy for all the trouble, demanded his dismissal. The bewildered king, having fled to Aranjuez before the French advance, mollified the mob by abdicating and proclaiming as king his son Ferdinand, who subsequently sent Godoy to prison. In a cynical chess game, Napoleon managed to abduct both old and new king, and the queen, to French territory. After a fast exchange of abdications and counterstatements, enlivened by the vile language of the queen, they all became victims of Napoleon's ambitious and complicated schemes which ended with Ferdinand a prisoner on French soil, and Charles, the queen and Godoy, a miserable trio of exiles in Rome. By Napoleon's order his brother Joseph, King of Naples since 1805, was now proclaimed King José I of Spain. The Spanish rose in arms against all oppression past and present. Signal for the long and bloody outburst were the massacres of the Second and Third of May (Slide 17). Suppressed for so long, the people raged against everything, the vestiges of Godoy's regime, the church, as well as the French invaders. Chaos reigned for six years and the disasters of war affected the whole land. In 1812 General Arthur Wellesley, first Duke of Wellington, entered Madrid in triumph at the head of a liberating English army, and was portrayed by Goya as the "terror Gallorum" (Figure 9). So rapid were the changes of power that Goya had to transform an equestrian portrait of the short-term king, Joseph, on which he was working at the time, into a hasty portrait of the "Iron Duke," as recent X-rays of the picture indicate (Wellington Museum, Apsley House, London). Even more telling as a political barometer is Goya's so-called "Allegory of the Town of Madrid" (Figure 10). Ordered by the City Council "from the best painter" and begun

Figure 9.
The Duke of Wellington (1812)
oil on canvas, 47½″ x 32⅞″
National Gallery of Art
Washington, D.C., gift of Mrs.
P. H. B. Frelinghuysen

in 1810 as a large scale tribute to the Intruder King, "our Sovereign," it showed Madrid, personified as a lovely woman, amidst all the trappings of fame and honor, pointing to a medallion containing the likeness of Joseph Bonaparte. After the liberation of 1812 the portrait was quickly painted out and substituted for it was the word "Constitución," in honor of the provisional, constitutional government that lasted less than a year and was replaced, in Madrid as well as in the picture, by the returning usurper. This second portrait was covered up again following political events in favor of the Constitution, and was succeeded subsequently by a portrait of Ferdinand VII, when the latter was released from French captivity and returned to the Spanish throne in 1814. The political situation (Ferdinand having just regained power again after another French invasion), as well as a change of taste, is indicated by the next layer of overpaint: Vicente López, alas, a dry and academic portraitist, succeeding the retired Goya in public and royal favor, added a more modern portrait of Ferdinand in 1823, which again, in reflection of political events was replaced by a reference to the Constitution in 1842. Soon afterwards historic interest prompted the removal of all layers to uncover Goya's very first original. This version, however, could no longer be rescued, whereupon the fateful date of "Dos de Mayo," the Second of May, was painted into the much abused medallion.

Goya's role during all these tragedy-ridden years remains dubious. Romantic legend makes him the patriotic hero but the facts reveal him as a turncoat of the swiftest order. During the reign of the Intruder King he painted marvelous portraits of members of the French oppression, acted on the difficult commission of selecting Spanish masterpieces of painting for Napoleon's museum in Paris (which were never sent), and received Joseph's Order of Spain, ridiculed as the "Egg Plant." His two great, historic canvases, the *Second of May* or *The Charge of the Mamelukes,* and the *Third of May* were painted six years after the fact, when the air was clear once more and accused collaborators needed rehabilitation. Only many years later was his etched diary of the fateful years published. The eighty etchings in the series of *Los Desastres de la Guerra* were inspired by incidents witnessed by the artist in the years 1808 to 1814, and represent a moving account of Goya's personal agony as well as a potent, timeless anti-war statement.

Goya's indictment of war is as obvious today as the meaning of some of his *Caprichos* is obscure. *Los Caprichos,* a series likewise comprising eighty plates of etchings, were published by Goya in 1799. These nightmarish visions had a harmless enough beginning. While spending happy months during the winter and spring of 1797 with the Duchess of Alba in Andalusia (Slide 11), Goya filled a small sketchbook, the so-called Sanlúcar Album, with intimate scenes of daily life, many of them featuring the slim-waisted duchess. After his return to Madrid he continued to draw from memory, into a larger sketchbook, scenes and observations which became increasingly satirical and led to the caustic caricatures of the *Caprichos.* While painting the glorious frescoes of San Antonio in 1798, he was preparing, at the same time, the copperplates for these startling etchings. On February 6, 1799, he advertised their publication in the "Diario de Madrid" with a lengthy text describing them as a criticism of "human errors and vices," as a ridicule of follies and wrongdoings common

Figure 10.
Allegory of the Town of Madrid
(begun 1810)
oil on canvas
102½″ x 76¾″
City Hall, Madrid
Photograph courtesy of MAS, Barcelona

to society and of "popular prejudices and lies authorized by custom, ignorance or interest." So carefully did he disclaim any reference in his text to particular persons, that one indeed suspects the mocking allusions to royalty, government, and well-known persons with which these *Caprichos* have always been credited. They are timely lampoons on modes and mores in the vein of the English satirist Hogarth, essays in the art of physiognomy, which had become the fashionable rage through the publications of the Swiss Protestant minister Lavater, products of the Age of Reason. On plate 43 (Figure 11), originally intended as the frontispiece for *Los Caprichos,* Goya shows himself asleep, beset by a hovering cast of evil-looking beasts, owls and bats. The inscription reads: "The Sleep of Reason produces Monsters," and in Goya's further explanation (from a handwritten document still preserved in the Prado): "Imagination, deserted by reason, produces impossible monsters. United with reason, she is the mother of all arts, and the source of their wonders." It is this clearly stated polarity between reason and imagination, one belonging to the rationalism of the eighteenth century, and the other to the romanticism of the early nineteenth century, that pervades all of Goya's work, most especially the *Caprichos*. These etchings, in fact, combine a social satire on contemporary human follies with a series of "dreams" attacking witchcraft and superstitions, in the name of truth. Small wonder that the *Caprichos* as a whole elude systematic interpretation. Having sold only twenty-seven sets by 1803, mostly to old friends and discerning foreigners, Goya gave the etched plates and 240 unsold sets of the edition to the crown, perhaps a gesture wisely calculated to avoid the Inquisition's too suspicious scrutiny of the meaning of some of the plates. Obviously, Goya's pungent tract on his time was a complete commercial flop. Artistically, however, the *Caprichos* soon became his best known masterpiece. Although we do not understand the contemporary puns intended, we can find universal meaning in his sharp observations of human nature. Goya's technical use of the media of etching and aquatint is unlike that of any other graphic artist working at the time. His flat shapes of light and dark, with which he expresses the essence of a scene more dramatically than with the rather banal subtitles to the plates, are as arresting and modern today as they were prophetic in his own era.

The popularity of the *Caprichos* is also partly based on their sarcastic humor. Such subjects as a prostitute caught in the cold, or donkeys studying their genealogies, are certainly more entertaining than the bitter illustrations of the *Disasters of War*. The latter are more moving, but less famous. After the financial failure of the *Caprichos,* Goya refrained from publishing the *Disasters,* and they were not printed until 1863, long after his death. Perhaps also the gruesome subject matter, "The fatal consequences of Spain's bloody war with Bonaparte and other striking observations," was too vivid in everyone's memory. The first part of the *Disasters* deals with the inglorious aspects of war, the horrors of shootings and stabbings, murders and massacres, bereavement and burials, of rape and flight, of female courage and anonymous heroism. On a heap of dead soldiers and civilians, a dying man, blood pouring from his mouth, is about to fall. The caption reads: "This is what you were born for." In another etching a man and a woman stare horrified at a pile of corpses, robbed even of their clothing: "Bury them and keep quiet," (Figure 12). War and battle illus-

Figure 11.
The Sleep of Reason produces Monsters
"Los Caprichos", plate 43
(about 1797-1799)
etching and aquatint, 8⁷⁄₁₆" x 5⁷⁄₈"
Prints Division, New York Public
Library, Astor, Lenox and Tilden
Foundations

Figure 12.
Bury Them and Keep Quiet
"Los Desastres de la Guerra", plate 18
(about 1810-1812)
etching and aquatint, 6¼" x 9¼"
Prints Division, New York Public Library
Astor, Lenox and Tilden Foundations

Figure 13.
*King Ferdinand VII
in Coronation Robes*
(1814), oil on canvas
83½″ x 57½″
Prado, Madrid

24

Figure 14.
Self Portrait (1815)
oil on canvas, 18⅛″ x 13¾″
Prado, Madrid

Figure 15.
Rembrandt Harmensz van Rijn
Self Portrait (1669)
oil on canvas, 23¼″ x 20″

trations, usually intent on historical detail and victorious sentiment, are rarely great art and seldom, if ever, moving. Goya's indignant, direct, unsentimental and artless response is heartbreaking. "Yo lo vi" (I saw it), the title of one scene, is the bitter motto for all plates. He also experienced the grim famine of 1811-12 that caused the death of thousands in Madrid and forms the subject of the second part of the *Disasters*. The third part moves from the hideous reality into a fantasy world, and is a series of political and religious satires more biting than the *Caprichos*.

With the war over, Goya went on making portraits, drawings and prints with uninterrupted productivity. Reinstated as Painter to the King, he painted in little more than a year no less than four portraits of Ferdinand VII for whom he bore nothing but hatred and disgust, and whom he depicts as mean, base and vain (Figure 13). What Goya himself looked like is shown in his self-portrait, dating from 1815 (Figure 14). At age seventy he appeared surprisingly robust and vigorous. This is the man who had sadly written to Zapater in 1787: "I have become old with so many wrinkles in my face that you would no longer recognize me if it were not for my flat nose and deepset eyes"; who had suffered repeated illnesses, and written to the king in 1798: "I am left so deaf that without the use of hand signs I cannot understand anything at all." Rembrandt, in a comparable self-portrait (Figure 15), is barely sixty but seems much older. Both men look at us with the same dark, knowing

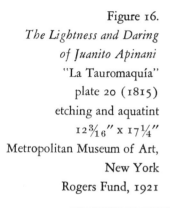

Figure 16.
The Lightness and Daring of Juanito Apinani
"La Tauromaquía"
plate 20 (1815)
etching and aquatint
12¾₁₆" x 17¼"
Metropolitan Museum of Art,
New York
Rogers Fund, 1921

eyes ringed in shadow, eyes that have seen so much but are without bitterness. Isolation and disillusionment did not rob these men of their zest for life, nor their creative spirits. Goya knew Rembrandt's graphic work well and acknowledged his indebtedness. It is documented that he himself owned prints by Rembrandt and borrowed others from the Biblioteca Nacional for study. Although his themes were very different, he learned technical mastery from Rembrandt's drawings and prints.

About 1815, at the time of the self-portrait, Goya began his etchings for *La Tauromaquía*, a series devoted to the art of bullfighting. Published in 1816, the thirty-three plates (later enlarged to forty) met with as little success as the *Caprichos*, but like them, became known and admired in the second half of the nineteenth century, especially in France. *La Tauromaquía* illustrates the origins and history of the popular Spanish sport and leads up to the spectacular stunts performed by Goya's contemporaries (Figure 16). Goya's eye was as quick as a camera, and he was miraculously capable of recording instantaneous movement. With strong contrasts of light and dark and stark concentration on the main features of the fight or deed, he achieved impressive effects. His love for the fiesta shows itself again ten years later in the famous *Bulls of Bordeaux*, four superb lithographs, in which the old man experimented with the new technique of prints made from drawings on stone, invented by the German Senefelder in 1796. In one of them (Figure 17) he marvelously intensifies the vigorous

Figure 17.
The Famous American,
Mariano Ceballos
"The Bulls of Bordeaux" (1825)
lithograph, 12¼″ x 15⅞″
Metropolitan Museum of Art
New York
Rogers Fund, 1920

Figure 18.
The Duel (about 1820)
sepia wash drawing
7½″ x 5⁵⁄₁₆″
Prado, Madrid

qualities of a plate from *La Tauramoquía*: the famous American, Mariano Ceballos, mounted on one bull fighting another. Ceballos, also known as the Indian, came to Spain from South America and died in the bull ring in 1780. Whether or not Goya had witnessed his daring almost fifty years earlier, the lithograph of Ceballos challenging the bull with his short spear shows the quivering excitement of something just seen.

Goya always made drawings as first notations of his inventive thoughts, mostly in preparation for his etchings. Done in various media, with brush or pen in ink or wash, in red or black chalk or in pencil, they steadily progress from the first weak copies after Velázquez to the highest peak of assured draftsmanship. In his mature years, drawings are no longer all preparatory studies. Often they serve him as the perfect and easiest means of direct self-expression. He renders reality and fantasy with equal precision through astoundingly few but telling lines and strokes (Figure 18). In front of these luminous masterpieces one is reminded both of Rembrandt and of Chinese brush drawings.

Slowly and almost imperceptibly, with undiminished artistic powers, Goya's life faded into old age. It was not his total deafness—so strong-willed a man had learned to cope with that—which separated him from the world around him. Witness to the coming and going of kings whose regimes his liberal mind opposed, and to the disappearance by death and exile of old friends and patrons, he more and more withdrew from public life. His wife had died in 1812, and his children before her. The only surviving son, Javier, had married in 1805, and the lonely old man doted on him, his new in-laws and his little grandson Mariano, all of whom he painted. Having suffered another acute and dangerous illness in 1819, he retired to the little house by the Manzanares which he had just bought, and for the next three years painted the most ghoulish, frightening visions on its walls (Slide 18 and Figure 19). In these Black Paintings he gave expression to the mysterious and demoniacal forces that had accrued in the depth of his being over a long lifetime. Considering the artist's age of seventy-four, and the lifesize scale of the fourteen murals alone, this series represents a gigantic task. In their total break with tradition they anticipate our modern art. Goya himself anticipates the modern artist. No longer serving a society that used to employ him, he sets himself apart and becomes free to give unrestrained expression to his own spirit and imagination.

At the same time and with the same disregard he etched the twenty-two large plates of the *Disparates* in the broad, massive style characteristic of his late period. When published in 1864, long after Goya's death, they were thought to illustrate proverbs and entitled *Los Proverbios*. Goya himself called them *Disparates* or follies, comments on the absurdities in human nature and behavior. Whatever their sometimes enigmatic meanings, their large-scale, sinister, and often monstrous figures powerfully silhouetted against dark backgrounds have a frightening and disquieting impact (Figure 20).

A revolt against the oppressive government of Ferdinand VII in 1820 had gained only short-lived constitutional freedom for Spain. In 1823 French troops invaded again, this time to restore the absolute monarchy. Liberals who escaped arrest fled in droves across the

Figure 19.
The Meeting of the Witches
(about 1821-1822), mural
transferred to canvas
55⅛" x 172½"
Prado, Madrid

Figure 20.
Ridiculous Folly
"Los Proverbios", plate 3
(about 1816-1824)
etching and aquatint
14¹⁄₁₆" x 18⅛"
Metropolitan Museum of Art, New York
Harris Brisbane Dick Fund, 1924

border. Goya also felt unsafe and went into hiding for a while. Then, after having made over his house and belongings to his son and grandson, he formally requested permission for a leave of absence as court painter under the pretext of needing to take the cure at Plombières in France. Instead, he went to Bordeaux, a haven for Spanish exiles and emigrants. There he was greeted by his old friend, the poet and dramatist Moratín, exiled since 1814, who wrote: "Goya has arrived, deaf, old, awkward and weak, not knowing a word of French, but happy as a lark and eager to see the world." After a few days, Goya went straight to Paris. Thanks to the suspicious French, the Paris police kept an eye on him, and reported that he stayed in his rented rooms most of the time, going out "only to see the sights of the city and roam the streets." One would like to know the sights he sought and the impression made on him by the Salon of 1824, in which works by Delacroix and landscapes by Constable were exhibited. No one in Paris seems to have been aware of the presence of the great Spanish master who, instead of roaming about alone, should have been carried through the streets in triumph by the younger generation. Classicism, the official art of Goya's period, so completely foreign to him and totally disregarded by him, had been swept under by the rising wave of Romanticism, yet the revolutionary work of its great prophet was then hardly known to the French painters who later admired him so much.

After two months Goya returned to Bordeaux and settled there together with his housekeeper, Leocadia Weiss, and her little daughter Rosario, for whom he showed as much affection as if she were his own, which might well have been the case. Once or twice he

31

returned to Madrid to renew his leave of absence. During one of these short stays, upon the king's order, the new court painter López portrayed the venerable artist in an honest though uninspired picture that, nevertheless, strikingly expresses in the sad, Rembrandtesque features, Goya's fierce determination and stubborn will (Figure 21). Indeed, as Goya himself wrote in 1825, he had an excess of will to live and work: "I may be like Titian, who lived to be ninety-nine." He proudly signed his penetrating portraits of friends "at the age of eighty" or "at the age of eighty-one." "Aún aprendo" (I am still learning) reads the title on a drawing of an old man walking on crutches. It might be an autobiographical reflection, for in Bordeaux he took up the new technique of lithography with superb results, painted miniatures on ivory in a loose, very modern style and opposed a new edition of the *Caprichos* because he had newer ideas now. After a much enjoyed visit from his daughter-in-law and grandson in 1828, he fell fatally ill and died on April 16, aged eighty-two.

No written epitaph can do justice to Goya's genius. Fortunately for us, he left his own in the vast amount of paintings, drawings and graphic works that bear witness to one of the greatest and most complex artists the world has ever known. He stands out in the wasteland of Spanish eighteenth and nineteenth century art leaving behind neither school nor pupils except for a few imitators and forgers. Not only was he an observer depicting the Spain of his days in all its throbbing, varied aspects, but he was also a fervent moralist who exposed the radical evil in human nature to all mankind. He was a brilliant artist who handled his tools with stunning effects that excite the eye, but he was also a great man who, like Titian, Rembrandt and Cézanne, in selfish solitude and through illness, sufferings, and compassionate anguish, pursued his art to its last consequence.

Figure 21.
Vicente López, *Portrait of Goya*
(1826), oil on canvas, 36½" x 30¼"
Prado, Madrid

1: CONDESA DE CHINCHÓN, María Teresa de Bourbon y Vallabriga (1783)
oil on canvas, 51" x 45½", Collection of Mrs. Mellon Bruce
Photograph courtesy of the National Gallery of Art, Washington, D. C.

Goya's commission to paint the Count of Floridablanca, chief minister of state, opened doors to the highest court circles and marked the beginning of Goya's career as portraitist. In that year, 1783, he was introduced to the brother of King Charles III, the Infante Don Luis de Bourbon, who commanded him to paint his family.

The youngest son of Philip V and Elisabeth Farnese, Don Luis seems to have been deliberately kept out of Bourbon family politics. Church titles had been heaped on him while he was still a child, but he renounced them all and, late in life, married María Teresa Vallabriga y Rosas, a beautiful young woman who came from an old Aragonese family. Because the marriage was considered a misalliance, Don Luis had to relinquish most of his royal privileges; María Teresa was never allowed to live at court. Thus, they lived practically in exile on the Infante's country estate at Arenas de San Pedro near Avila, where Goya spent over a month, painting his hosts and their three children and becoming an intimate friend of the family.

The little daughter, named María Teresa after her mother, is portrayed here at the age of two years and nine months according to the inscription at the lower left. Her imperious pose and grown-up dress contrast charmingly with the tiny figure and innocent, open face of the child. The blue-grey Sierra de Gredos dominates the background, reminding one of the mountains in Velázquez' portrait of the Infante Baltasar Carlos in the Prado, which is similar in many aspects and must have influenced this composition. The rendering is broad and colorful as in Goya's tapestry cartoons, and most delightful as pure and free painting with light and liquid brushstrokes.

This enchanting child was to have a tragic future. Queen María Luisa arranged her marriage with her own notorious lover, Manuel Godoy, Prince of the Peace, and forced her to live an unhappy existence at the court. Goya portrayed her again in 1800, in one of his most appealing portraits, after she had been given the title of Countess of Chinchón. When Godoy fell from power in 1808 and fled with the royal family to France, she left him and went to live with her brother, the Cardinal of Toledo. She died in 1828.

2: THE MARQUESA DE PONTEJOS (about 1786), oil on canvas, 83" x 49¾"
National Gallery of Art, Washington, D. C., Andrew Mellon Collection

The portrait of the young Marquesa de Pontejos illustrates perfectly the French modes and manners of the Rococo that ruled the upper classes of Spanish society in the 1780's. Delicate as a Meissen porcelain figure, she stands posed as if on the stage of Marie Antoinette's private theater at Versailles. Her costume is as affected as her pose for she is dressed as a shepherdess, according to the fashionable ideas of a return to nature, as preached by Jean Jacques Rousseau. She is, however, a very elegant shepherdess with ruffles, frills and ribbons, her hair lightly powdered and topped by an enormous straw hat adorned with fluffy tulle. Her costume is a marvel of shimmering silver-greys and pinks, accentuated by the carnation she so primly holds. Hinting at rusticity there are a few artificial-looking daisies in the foreground, and in the place of sheep a droll little pug dog with a collar of bells and pink ribbons. The background is simply a foil, like a theatrical set, painted in the same light hues as the backgrounds of Goya's tapestry cartoons.

With all its pretty artificiality, this is one of the most enchanting portraits Goya ever painted. It must have pleased the young lady and all who saw it, but Goya never painted anything so lighthearted again in his life.

Doña María Ana de Pontejos y Sandovel, Countess of la Ventosa and Marchioness of Pontejos, was about twenty years old at the time of this portrait. It was probably painted on the occasion of her marriage in 1786 to the brother of the all-powerful Count of Floridablanca, who undoubtedly recommended Goya for this picture. We know little else about the determined-looking girl beyond the fact that she was soon widowed and remarried to an officer in the king's bodyguard. Widowed again, she married in 1817 the rich Don Joaquín Vizcaino y Moles, founder of the Spanish Savings Bank. She died in 1834.

3: DON MANUEL OSORIO DE ZUÑIGA (also known as THE RED BOY) (1787-1788), oil on canvas, 50" x 40"
Metropolitan Museum of Art, New York, The Jules S. Bache Collection, 1949

This is one of the most appealing and successful portraits of children ever painted, and also one of the most famous. Immediately striking is the little boy's bright vermilion suit, a daring red, never before found so vibrant, so unmodulated in painting.

The child is fully identified by the inscription along the bottom of the picture which states that he was El Señor Don Manuel Osorio Manrique de Zuñiga, Señor de Gines, born in 1784. Since he appears to be about three or four years old, we might assume the portrait to be painted around 1787-1788. At that time Goya also painted portraits of the boy's father, the Count of Altamira, member of one of the noblest families of Spain; of his mother, posed stiffly on a sofa with her little daughter; and a charming, subtle likeness of his brother, then ten years old. Of these family portraits, that of Don Manuel is the outstanding one for its imagination and painterly skill, and for its unconventional directness and beauty of colors.

Untinged by the sweet sentimentality with which English painters imbued their children's portraits, the frail little boy stands alone and erect before a plain grey-green wall. His delicate face is transparent and pale in contrast to his luminous finery. Arms apart, he is holding a string attached to the foot of a magpie, a favorite children's pet since the Middle Ages. In his beak, the bird displays Goya's visiting card, decorated with palette, brushes and mahlstick, picked up from the floor where the artist dropped it to indicate his presence.

Don Manuel is not looking at us. Something else, outside of the picture, has arrested the gaze of his round, brown eyes for a pensive moment. All motion is suspended, but one can easily imagine all hell breaking loose in the next instant, when those monstrously intent cats, foreboding evil, jump at the magpie and tear apart the fragile birdcage, creating disorder and early sorrow. We do not know what happened to Don Manuel in later life, but we know that soon afterwards the French Revolution started the upheaval of the ancient social order all over Europe. By introducing the dark forces of evil Goya gave poignancy to his portrayal of innocent youth.

4: THE FAMILY OF THE DUKE OF OSUNA (about 1789)
oil on canvas, 88″ x 68″, Prado, Madrid

The Dukes of Osuna, enormously rich for generations, had used their wealth to become great gentlemen and patrons of the arts. The ninth duke, a kindly and generous man, was no exception: his collection of paintings by Goya, of which he owned at least twenty-five, was second only to that of the king. This may have been due as much or more to the taste and predilections of his wife, the Duchess of Bonavente, who was just as rich as her husband and apparently quite charmed by Goya, the man as well as his paintings. She was considered not only the proudest woman in Spain and a social rival of the beautiful Duchess of Alba, but one of the best dressed women in all of Europe.

The portrait of the Osuna family bears a striking resemblance to a painting by Gainsborough of the Baillie Family, done about 1784 and now in the Tate Gallery in London. It has often been suggested that English portrait painting, which flourished so brilliantly during the second half of the eighteenth century, may have influenced the work of Goya. He was probably aware of the style of Gainsborough, Reynolds and Romney, through engravings and the popular colored mezzotints which may have reached Spain, but no convincing connections have been established so far and the analogies are of generic character. The Baillie Family and the Osuna Family portraits are both composed of the seated mother, the father who stands beside her chair, and four children, loosely grouped in a shallow space and most of them looking at the spectator. But while the Baillie portrait is permeated by flowing lines and an easy grace, which give it elegance and a restful timelessness, Goya's portrait is full of sudden angles and an awkward stiffness, which makes it all the more arresting, if not disturbing.

The Osuna portrait has often been dismissed as feeble, but on the contrary, it is a subtle masterpiece. It is the portrayal of a happy, young family, without sentimentalism, without loss of their aristocratic distinction, without artful compositional devices, seen realistically and painted in the most beautiful light and muted hues.

5: THE MANIKIN (1791), oil on canvas, 105″ x 63″, Prado, Madrid

Had Goya died at the age of forty-five, when he painted this tapestry cartoon in 1791, he would be known, if at all, chiefly for his sixty-three designs for the Royal Tapestry Factory of Santa Bárbara, and these might be considered strangely scurrilous and rather provincial works. Most likely they would have remained rolled up, as they were for so many years, in some basement and would have deteriorated beyond repair. As in the case of Cézanne, whose work also came to full fruition only in mature years, the mastery of the late years was needed to reflect glory and significance on the early achievements.

In this cartoon, four young women are tossing a dummy in a blanket, a carefree theme that Goya's contemporary Fragonard might have treated with the charm and wit of the French Rococo. Goya's women would be judged a bit stiff and their grins stupid if we had not learned from subsequent works, especially the etchings of the *Caprichos*, how to understand them. The harmless pastime is represented as a caustic lampoon on the fickleness of women who, with witchlike glee, toss about the grotesque jumping jack, an equivocal image of man. The background is barely indicated, and in the hazy landscape the women and their victim stand out clearly and effectively.

"The Manikin" is the cartoon—actually an oil painting on canvas—for one of the tapestries from a series of four to be woven for the king's study in the Escorial, now in the Prado Museum, and was Goya's last commission for the factory. Since his first cartoons of 1776, he had learned to consider the technique of tapestry weaving, and to create designs that could be executed by the weavers without too much difficulty. This meant flat colors with as little gradation as possible, simplified forms and avoidance of deep perspective. Work within these limitations proved to be excellent training for Goya in achieving bold results with simple means. Also, the subject matter of the tapestries, chosen by the king to represent the "costumes and diversions of the time" influenced him fundamentally, because in a wider context, this became the basic theme for all his work.

6: DON SEBASTIÁN MARTÍNEZ (signed and dated 1792), oil on canvas 36⅝″ x 26⅝″, Metropolitan Museum of Art, New York, Rogers Fund, 1906

The likeness of Don Sebastián Martínez shows a refined elegance in pose and color scheme that appears less Spanish than French. Yet it is not known where Goya could have seen portraits by Greuze or Madame Vigée-Lebrun that might have influenced such sophistication in the delicate contrast between the shimmering silk coat, striped in blue and green, and the modish yellow knee breeches, the impeccable wig with its one curl and the intelligent expression of the man looking up from the study of a drawing. The sheet of paper is inscribed with Goya's dedication of the portrait to his friend, and it must have been, at least in part, the urbanity of the sitter that inspired this perfect portrayal of the enlightened eighteenth century gentleman.

Don Sebastián (1747-1800) was a lawyer and the general treasurer of the financial council in Cadíz. His ample income allowed him to become a connoisseur and collector of art, and he assembled a fine group of books, prints, and about 300 paintings, among them works attributed to Titian, Velázquez and Leonardo da Vinci. Cadíz was a flourishing harbor town linked by trade with England and France, and more cosmopolitan than most Spanish cities. The houses of the rich merchants were filled with art from other countries, and Goya surely welcomed this opportunity to see and study their collections. Goya and Martínez shared friends in Saragossa, which may have prompted Goya's visit to Cadíz in 1792, to which our portrait bears witness. A short time later, Goya suffered the strange illness which affected the rest of his life. In 1793 he stayed again with Martínez for several months of convalescence. This portrait marks the end of the first and mundane period of Goya, the Rococo artist, the socially successful portraitist and designer of royal tapestries.

7: THE BURIAL OF THE SARDINE (1793), oil on wood
32½" x 24¼", Academia de San Fernando, Madrid

Shrove Tuesday, the last day of Carnival before Ash Wednesday and the beginning of Lent, was celebrated in Madrid in the old days, as it still is today in Rio and New Orleans, with exuberant parades, masquerades, and licentious indulgences. It was "the Tuesday for eating meat" before forty days of fast and abstinence. The traditional title for this picture "The Burial of the Sardine" is unexplained, but one can well imagine a pun enjoyed by people who for weeks to come had to live on sardines, the staple food for the lower classes in Spain and Portugal all year around.

Aware of the deep human insight of Goya's work and its satirical aspects, we are apt to read too much into this genre scene of gay revelry. Nevertheless, one only has to compare it with one of Giovanni Domenico Tiepolo's carnival scenes of Venice, the city of eternal carnival, to realize its Goyesque character and disturbing meaning. In Tiepolo's pictures the harlequins' costumes and elegant fancy dresses evoke a world of carefree pleasure, of fantasy, music and dance. The masked dancers in Goya's picture, however, as awkwardly stiff as puppets on a string, seem to lead a dance of death. Their folly is real, desperate and macabre. The composition is dominated by the banner with its smiling mask, looming large above the mad crowd. The grin on the mask's face is frightening, sadistic, and knowing: all this festivity will come to a terrible end.

No longer individuals behind their masks, these are human masses as anonymous as the mob that marched on Versailles a few years earlier, in 1789. They encircle the light center of the picture, and extend as far as one can see. With short, agitated strokes, Goya has captured their jerky, grotesque movements. Subject matter and technique are united in a new style that is highly original and more modern than anything else painted at the time.

8:   THE MADHOUSE (1794 or after), oil on wood, 17¾" x 28⅜"
Academia de San Fernando, Madrid

Barely recovered from the paralyzing illness that had left him deaf for life, Goya wrote to Don Bernardo de Iriarte, Vice-protector of the Real Academia de Bellas Artes de San Fernando, in 1794: "To occupy my imagination, tormented by the contemplation of my ailments, and to compensate in part for the great expenses they have caused me, I have devoted myself to painting a number of cabinet pictures in which I have succeeded in making observations for which commissioned works give no opportunity and in which fantasy and invention have no room for expansion." Sending eleven such pictures, he added that one, which was not yet finished, represented a madhouse. The style and technique of this picture is so advanced as to point to a later date and most scholars hesitate to accept it as the one mentioned in the letter. However, Goya constantly surprises us with his jumps into the future or reminiscences of the past and makes it extremely difficult, if not often impossible, to place undated works in their probable sequence.

Coming out of his illness, he entered a world forever silent, and it is no wonder that his eyes were keener than ever in their awareness of his fellow men's sufferings and follies. He probably visited insane asylums to make the observations referred to in his letter, and later painted several other versions. The subject would obviously fascinate an artist of his interests. In the picture, huddled in the background, are some cloaked visitors watching the mad proceedings. It was considered quite entertaining in the eighteenth century to watch the lunatics in their snakepit, and the society of Paris flocked to nearby Charenton to see the inmates of the asylum perform plays written and directed by the Marquis de Sade, himself an inmate.

Here we see crowned emperors, a wild savage with feathers in his headband, a man trying to fit a bull's horns to his head. Stripped naked, locked in vast, arched dungeons, they are prisoners of their malady. Madness is seen as a horrific spectacle, just as Goya's festivals are spectacles of mad folly. There is a remarkable absence of the social or moral comment with which similar scenes by Goya's English counterpart Hogarth are charged. Loosely composed, painted in luminous, neutral tints of ochre and grey, this small picture is an acute description of man's shadow-land, merciless, painful, and as terrifying as a nightmare.

9: FRANCISCO BAYEU Y SUBIAS (1795), oil on canvas
44⅛" x 33⅛", Prado, Madrid

Francisco Bayeu's survival in the annals of art is due less to his own, generally undistinguished, achievements as a painter, than to his relationship with the young Goya whom he sponsored, and who became his brother-in-law. It is especially due, however, to this remarkable portrait of him by Goya. Born at Saragossa in 1734, he was Goya's senior by twelve years and preceded him to Madrid where honors and commissions were soon bestowed on him. In 1765 he became Court Painter, and in 1788, Director of the Royal Academy. After his death Goya succeeded him in both positions.

Bayeu died in August 1795, and his daughter commissioned the portrait posthumously. Goya set to work immediately and showed the picture in a still unfinished state at the Academy later in the same month. It follows closely Bayeu's own self portrait, now in a private collection in Madrid, which shows the artist seated, holding palette and brushes, in front of a canvas on which a neo-classical scene is sketched. Using the same conventional composition, Goya, with sheer magic, transformed the pedestrian original into one of his most masterly portraits. As in many portraits painted in the 1790s, shimmering greys and silvery tones dominate the color scheme. The touch of the brush is free, but also extremely delicate.

Goya suppressed all details and attributes of the painter's craft, except for the single brush. Its vertical position stresses Bayeu's erect and stern pose. While in his self portrait Bayeu looks thoroughly disagreeable, a bitter, suspicious, quarrelsome person, Goya, who had his own quarrels with him, penetrates through the mask of malice and shows us an unhappy and disappointed man. Despite great acclaim, and a large output of frescoes, oil paintings and cartoons for tapestries, Bayeu probably knew that, as an artist, he was inferior to Goya, and suffered most of his life under this knowledge. In following too closely the neo-classical ideals of Mengs and in feebly imitating Tiepolo's large decorative schemes he had become, as Pedro de Madrazo described him, "a fallen angel of art, through the denial of his own personality and his submission to a style against which all his natural talents rebelled in vain."

10: THE WITCHES' SABBATH, also known as *EL AQUELARRE* (about 1795-98)
oil on canvas, 17⅛" x 12⅛", Lázaro Galdiano Museum, Madrid

An enormous goat, crowned with laurels, the very incarnation of the devil, presides over a circle of old hags. A crescent moon is waxing, and black bats dot an ominous sky. Tiny embryos are hung on a stick, and dead children lie about. A skeletal child is offered for sacrifice, but the goat reaches for the well-fed baby in the arms of an imploring mother. "Goya, nightmare full of things unknown, of embryos which are roasted at a witches' sabbath, of old crones looking into the mirror, and children completely naked to tempt the demons. . . ." Thus the French poet Baudelaire, in his *Flowers of Evil* (1857), summed up his impression of Goya's frightening artistry, and partly described this picture. It is an early rendering of the supernatural, a subject that interested Goya throughout his career, and is more literally descriptive than later pictures where fantasy and horror are expressed through formal rather than iconographic means, as in the witch scenes of the Black Paintings.

The picture illustrates the widespread interest in witchcraft in Madrid toward the end of the eighteenth century, not only among the lower classes who are always subject to it, but especially among the upper classes. As a privileged society always seeks new thrills to substitute for gods in whom they can no longer believe, so the Spanish aristocracy, bored with the Age of Reason, found excitement in witchcraft and sorcery, which were dangerously attractive since such beliefs were persecuted by the Inquisition. It was the rich and worldly Duchess of Osuna who bought this picture, along with five other witch scenes, for the Osuna country residence, "La Alameda," south of Aranjuez.

Goya's extraordinary gift for visualizing monsters and scenes of diabolic happenings was equalled only by Hieronymus Bosch. There appears to be a very Spanish affinity for this sort of subject, for as much as the duchess favored Goya, so did King Philip II collect the works of his Dutch precursor who depicted the frightening world of the imagination.

11:   THE DUCHESS OF ALBA (1797), oil on canvas, 82¾" x 58¾"
Courtesy of the Hispanic Society of America, New York

Doña María Teresa Cayetana de Silva y Alvarez de Toledo was the thirteenth Duchess of Alba in her own right, and the most celebrated beauty of her day in Spain. When she was barely eleven years old, she was married to the eleventh Marquis of Villafranca, about whom little is known except that he was exceedingly rich and loved music. In his portrait by Goya, he leans on a clavichord holding a score by Haydn.

The duke died in Seville in 1796, and María Teresa retired for a short period of mourning to her Andalusian estates of Sanlúcar near Cadíz. Goya joined her, and painted there this magnificent portrait of her. Against a background of toned-down hues reminiscent of the tapestry cartoons, a greyish-blue sky, grey trees, a pinkish stream crossing the middle distance, a grey-green foreground, she stands imperiously, a Spaniard and an aristocrat from top to toe. Her dress is resplendent simply by virtue of the artist's brilliant brushwork. The black skirt sparkles with ribbons, the golden-yellow bodice gleams through the lacy mantilla, and a red sash fringed with gold, encircles her fashionably slim waist. White slippers embroidered with gold match the bow of white and yellow ribbons placed in a mass of dark, curly hair. The large eyes under the heavy black eyebrows command our attention, as does the prominently placed hand adorned with two large rings bearing the names "Alba" and "Goya." The index finger points to the inscription facing her in the sand: "Solo Goya"—Goya alone.

Goya had fallen in love, and spent happy months with his hostess in the sunny country. The pages of his Sanlúcar sketchbook are filled with fresh and intimate observations of female beauty, inspired by the duchess. Yet the passion with which he laid claim to her person as expressed in this portrait, was not to last. Goya was about fifty-one years old and stone deaf; the duchess only thirty-five and independent and capricious. In a drawing for an unpublished etching in the Caprichos series, entitled "Dream of Lying and Inconstancy," he represented himself grasping the arm of the fickle, two-faced duchess, who extends her hand to other companions. Her features appear frequently again in later satirical drawings and etchings.

The Duchess of Alba died in 1802, some say mysteriously of poison. Had it not been for Goya's brush, this famous *femme fatale* would long since have been forgotten.

12: SAINT ANTHONY RAISING A DEAD MAN (1798), fresco
detail from the Church of San Antonio de la Florida, Madrid

A short walk from the Royal Palace, in the so-called Florida section, which in Goya's time bordered the northern outskirts of Madrid, stands the small church of San Antonio de la Florida. Not much larger than a chapel, it had been rebuilt in 1792 in the neo-classical style, and Goya received the royal command to decorate the interior with frescoes. Begun in the summer of 1798, and completed in a remarkably short time, supposedly in exactly 120 days, this fresco cycle is one of his most impressive, astounding and successful works. Apparently the king was also pleased, for as a result he appointed him First Painter to the King, the highest honor a Spanish painter could attain.

The church was dedicated to St. Anthony of Padua, and depicted here is the incident of St. Anthony raising a dead man to life in order that he might disclose the name of his murderer, and save the innocent man who is accused. This is a macabre theme, but Goya painted it in the most cheerful fashion imaginable. According to legend, the miracle took place in Lisbon in the thirteenth century, but Goya has set the scene in the Madrid of his own time. The little church is situated near the banks of the Manzanares river where the rich and the poor gathered for fresh air and fun. Goya recreates the miracle right there among them. Behind a painted railing, the fashionable men and women of Madrid society can be seen intermingling with a raucous crowd of distinctly lower class. Everybody behaves as he pleases while the Saint performs his miracle, paying less attention to him than they would to the spectacle of a wandering rope dancer.

The impact of the frescoes on the casual visitor is limited because they are painted high in the cupola and the spandrels of the narrow, dimly lit church. Since detailed photography has brought them closer to our eyes, however, we must marvel at the painter's sprightly imagination. Without elaborate preparatory drawings or oil sketches he painted freely and quickly on the wet plaster, with joyful, light colors that remind us of Tiepolo, and with an abbreviated technique and deft characterization that foreshadow the entire nineteenth century from Delacroix to the Impressionists. Although seen by few, the frescoes of San Antonio are perhaps Goya's greatest and most painterly achievement.

13: THE INFANTA DOÑA MARÍA JOSEFA (1800)
oil on canvas, 29¼" x 23½", Prado, Madrid

After the coveted appointment as First Painter to the Court in 1799, Goya received few royal commissions and those only during the next two years, although he boasted to his old correspondent Zapater: "The sovereigns are mad about your friend." In 1799, he painted four official portraits of the king and the queen, and in April 1800, the king wrote from his summer palace of Aranjuez that he wanted Goya to come and paint "all of us together." Goya went, and did preparatory oil sketches of the members of the family which are unequalled in their vigor and directness. Sketching rapidly in front of the sitter, probably in one short sitting, he did not allow anything extraneous to infringe on the fresh likeness. With unusual detachment and technical virtuosity he painted, as Frans Hals had done before him and Manet would later, just what he saw. The orange-red priming of the canvas enabled him to achieve lively flesh tones quickly with a few extremely liquid strokes of the brush.

This sketch shows María Josefa, the oldest daughter of Charles III and sister of King Charles IV. With the typically long nose of the Bourbon family and watery eyes, she appears a kindly old spinster. Not even the large beauty spot or "mouche," hiding a blemish or wart at her temple, nor the enormous dangling diamond earrings excite any social comment or detract from her humanity.

The lifelike quality of the sketch, as that of all the sketches of her relatives, is lost in the finished group portrait. Unmarried, the oldest person in the picture and not linked with politics as the others are, she is squeezed in the background, lurking with an owlish expression behind the shoulders of the younger generation (Figure 8). The center of the stage is demonstratively held by the queen, bedecked with jewels and surrounded by her children, of which she had many of both. Unkind critics have compared the group to the family of a small shopkeeper who had just won a prize in the lottery. It is true that this family was notably lazy and unintellectual, but they knew how to play their inherited roles well. What is missing in the simple composition are the pompous trappings, columns, steps, and draperies that were the customary embellishments of royal portraiture. Goya has made up for their absence by the splendour and sparkle of their jewels, orders, silks and ribbons, and given distinction to the assembly of shallow souls through the brilliant flourish of his brush, spattering golds, reds and blues all over and creating with consummate skill a symphony of colors and light.

This was Goya's biggest and best group portrait, including the thirteen royal personages and himself at the easel in the background. Although the monarchs were very pleased indeed, it was also to be his last royal commission.

14: MAJAS ON A BALCONY (1800-1805), oil on canvas, 76¾" x 49½"
Metropolitan Museum of Art, Bequest of Mrs. H. O. Havemeyer, 1929,
The H. O. Havemeyer Collection

The "Majas on a Balcony" is a splendid illustration of Spanish life in Goya's time. Then as now, the women spent many of their leisure hours on balconies, a common feature of Spanish houses designed for watching the passing street scene. Placing figures behind a balustrade is a most effective pictorial device which Goya had used before in his frescoes in San Antonio de la Florida. Manet, the French Impressionist painter, was much impressed by the composition and plainly copied it in his picture of two young Parisian women on a balcony accompanied by a jovial and dandyish gent. But what a difference between Manet's innocuous and mundane group, and Goya's alluring and slightly mysterious couples. Looming in the background like the sinister cats in the portrait of Don Manuel Osorio, two cloaked men hover over their lovely prey with a conspiratory air of which the spirited young women seem happily unaware. While one appears diverted by something she sees on the street below, the other is regarding us with a beautiful, cool stare, tapping her friend lightly on the arm to draw her attention.

In the inventory of Goya's effects drawn up in 1812 the picture is described simply as "Young people on a Balcony." Only later did the word "Maja" appear in the title. It is often thought to denote ladies of easy virtue, and their posing on a balcony in the company of such suspicious-looking fellows certainly seems to support this interpretation. Actually, the Maja and her male counterpart, the Majo, belonged to the artisan class of Madrid and distinguished themselves by their high spirits and by the ostentation and freedom of their dress. It was fashionable at that time for members of society to affect the dress of a Maja or Majo in opposition to the French manners and modes favored by the Bourbon court, either as an expression of national pride or simply for fun. These girls may well be aristocratic ladies in the disguise of Majas, and Goya gives us a hint of their amorous dalliance. Whatever their morals may have been, they are painted with extraordinary virtuosity. The sparkling embroidery of their dresses is done with thick pigment applied by rapid thrusts of the palette knife which contrasts with other parts of delicate transparency.

15: THE MAJA CLOTHED (before 1808), oil on canvas
37¼" x 74¾", Prado, Madrid

"La Maja Vestida," a young woman dressed in fancy national costume, is too often mistaken for one of Goya's masterpieces, while in fact her fame is based on extraneous circumstances. Arms lifted behind her head, she poses self-consciously on a bed of fluffy pillows, and looks at us with saucy allure. The plump shapes of her young body are exhibited fully and are emphasized rather than hidden by the clinging dress. Shimmering silks and laces are painted in wonderful shades of cool whites and greys, enlivened by the pink sash and the mustard-colored sleeves of the bolero.

The explanation for the painting's exaggerated fame—or better, notoriety—is to be found in its companion piece, a picture of the same model in virtually the same pose but undressed; further, in the scandalous, but legendary, assumption that the model was none other than one of the highest ranking ladies in Spanish aristocracy, the beautiful Duchess of Alba.

Too much fantasy has arisen around the romantic love affair between the painter and the duchess, which the two mistaken "Maja" paintings helped to seem more piquant. Napoleon's frivolous sister had shocked Roman society when she insisted that Canova portray her in the nude, but this was unthinkable in Spain, however wanton the little duchess may have been. Now scholars agree that the two infamous pictures were painted after her death, which occurred in 1802, and that her friendship with the painter had cooled several years before. However, to squelch the forever persistent rumor once and for all, the Alba family found it necessary to disinter their ancestor, and to produce the macabre evidence that her measurements did not correspond to those of the damsel depicted in the two compromising pictures. And yet, despite all proof to the contrary, visitors to the Prado will never stop whispering in front of them.

In their combination of dress and undress the two paintings create the impression of a private peep-show. Considering that the still powerful Inquisition prohibited virtually all representations of nudity, it might be true that the one picture was meant to cover the other, to be removed only on special occasions. Most likely they were painted for Manuel Godoy, the libertine Chief Minister of State, who was also one of Goya's most appreciative patrons. They are listed among his possessions after his downfall in 1808. The Inquisition finally caught up with them in 1815, when Goya was ordered to appear before the tribunal in regard to "two obscene paintings." His replies, if they were known, might have solved the mystery of the model, but would also have deprived the world of some entertaining gossip.

16: THE BULLFIGHT (about 1810), oil on canvas, 38¾" x 49¾"
The Metropolitan Museum of Art, New York, Wolfe Fund, 1922

Bullfighting is to the Spaniard what baseball is to the American. Considered cruel by the rest of the world, the *corrida* is essential to Spanish life. Godoy, the Prime Minister, hastened his own fall from power when he unwisely forbade all bullfights in 1805, and Joseph Bonaparte, briefly king after the French invasion, was quick to open the gates to the ring again in 1808. Goya was no less interested in the bullfight than his countrymen. One of the many legends which are attached to his youth is that he worked his way to the southern coast earning enough money for his passage to Rome by fighting the bull as a professional. In a letter to his friend Zapater he signed himself jokingly "Francisco de los Toros," and at the age of eighty he still proudly boasted that he had fought bulls in his younger years. He was a friend of the great matadors and painted portraits of several of them who were then, as they are now, the heroes of the people and the pets of society.

Such was the appetite for bullfights in Goya's time that often the arena was divided like a double-ring circus to allow two fights to take place simultaneously. In this picture, the excitement of the spectacle is expressed by the rapid, sketchy brushwork, indeed so sketchy, that many have declared the picture to be unfinished. To indicate movement, the swaying crowd, the heat and dust, the typical bullfight atmosphere, he has employed a shorthand of agitated strokes and quick touches that can be called impressionistic. Whoever has seen a bullfight knows the dramatic effect of sun and shade in the arena, which Goya has brought into full play in the composition of the picture, contrasting darker and lighter masses.

17:   THE THIRD OF MAY (1814), oil on canvas
104¾″ x 136″, Prado, Madrid

On the second and third of May, 1808, two bloody events sparked the Spanish War of Independence. Napoleon's general Murat and his troops occupied Madrid, while Charles IV, who had abdicated under the force of unruly circumstances, the queen and her favorite Godoy, as well as the new king, Ferdinand VII, had been abducted across the border to France. When the youngest prince, Francisco, a favorite with the people, was to be moved from the Royal Palace to France at Napoleon's command, there was a small incident involving some women screaming, and a gathering crowd that surrounded the waiting carriage and attacked the French escort. Shots were fired, and in a short time the fiery temperament of the Spaniards raged in wild fury against the hated invaders. Murat acted quickly and sent his famous Egyptian Mamelukes to the Puerta del Sol, Madrid's main square, where they brutally butchered the assembled, mostly unarmed, crowd. The night and day following the blood bath, everyone who carried arms or simply looked patriotic was dragged up to the hill of Principe Pio outside the city, and shot by firing squads.

The massacres inspired Goya's two largest history paintings. Yet, by comparison, "The Second of May" is an artistic failure, lacking in impact and conviction, while its companion piece, "The Third of May," is one of the world's great masterpieces of painting.

Legend has it that Goya witnessed the events. A lukewarm collaborator under the French regime, he painted the massacres six years later, almost like a plea for rehabilitation. However, the picture of the shooting of May 3rd has the impact of an experience actually felt, of an instantaneous action seen and immediately set down. Unlike other paintings celebrating historical events, there is no rhetoric, no contrived symbolism, no traditional pictorial formula, no stale studio atmosphere. In fact, no studies for the great canvas exist. The brutality of the scene is conveyed with brutal directness and simplicity. Although the picture contains many figures, we perceive mainly two: the uniformed French soldier ready to fire, an anonymous power multiplied in a row of similar, angular, almost abstract shapes, and the Spaniard in the white shirt, his arms thrown up in a violent gesture of defiance and despair, the gesture implying a sort of profane crucifixion. It is an unforgettable figure, embodying the long agony of the Spanish people.

A lantern on the ground illuminates the scene of horror like footlights on the stage of the Grand Guignol, creating a dramatic pattern of dark and light. As we look longer, we recognize the shapeless bodies of the dead, the quivering mass of those facing the rifles, and the new batch of victims pushed uphill like animals to the slaughter. Like a news reporter, Goya captured the flash of a single moment. At the same time he painted a permanent statement that is a grim reflection on oppression and revolution, on armed power and patriotic suffering.

18: SATURN DEVOURING A SON (1819-1823), oil on plaster
transferred to canvas, 57½" x 32¾", Prado, Madrid

This is one of the most aggressively disturbing paintings in the whole history of western art. It is as brutally frank as the "Guernica" by Picasso, or anything painted by Francis Bacon. Moreover, its uncompromising impact is timeless. When the Black Paintings were shown to the public for the first time in Paris at the World's Fair of 1878, an English artist and critic, P. G. Hamerton, wrote enraged: "Of all these things the most horrible is the *Saturn.* He is devouring one of his children with the voracity of a famished wolf, and not a detail of the disgusting feast is spared you. The figure is a real inspiration, as original as it is terrific, and not a cold product of mere calculating design." The puritanical indignation which spurred Hamerton's essay on the base and repugnant nature of Goya, the man and his work, unwillingly praised the picture to today's viewer. We do not have to know its mythological content to be gripped by anxiety and a disturbing notion of the unpleasant truth. As Rembrandt's late pictures ask us questions about ourselves, this one startles us into regions of our consciousness rarely admitted to exist.

"Saturn" was one of the fourteen frescoes with which Goya decorated the two main rooms of his country house, the "Quinta del Sordo" (House of the Deaf Man), which he bought in 1819, and made over to his grandson in 1823, prior to his departure for France. In what a morbid state his spirits must have been when the lonely, seventy-four year old artist created these frightening Black Paintings on the inner walls of his pretty, pink and white stucco villa. Their name, Black Paintings, is a rather recent one, but describes them well. Not only are they painted mostly in black, but they convey a black mood, a black humor. Many have tried to explain their obscure meanings without success. They represent Goya's own demoniacal inner world.

Of all the frescoes, "Saturn" is the easiest to explain. Rubens had painted the same subject in a series of decorations for a royal hunting lodge, the Torre de la Parada. Amongst other paintings of mythical gods and goddesses, the lord of the Titans, Cronus, or as he was known in Latin, Saturn, is eating his new-born children since he had been warned that his sons would dethrone him; his son Zeus escaped the gruesome fate and eventually managed to do so. Rubens painted the repulsive scene with all the baroque indulgence in sensual excess. By Goya's time, his canvas of 1636 hung in the Royal Palace where the artist must have seen it often. Rubens' illustration of an ancient myth, however, is worlds apart from the violent image that Goya painted on his wall to be a daily reminder of man's true nature. The intense action of frightened eating, the intemperate ugliness of jarring limbs, and the undisguised sensual excitement border on the ludicrous. This seeming lack of artistry that repelled art lovers of the past, now has its direct, passionate effect on us who have learned to stomach much, and sense its message of violence and depravity.

19: DON RAMÓN SATUÉ (signed and dated 1823), oil on canvas
41" x 32", The Rijksmuseum, Amsterdam

A late work, this is one of Goya's most modern portraits, a timeless and powerful portrayal of man and his humanity. No more shimmering brocades, laces, medals, and gilded furniture, no more decorative pleasantries. By comparison with this, Goya's portraits of the eighteenth century seem like figures from a fairyland. The world has changed, and we are here face to face with a new reality. He is not posed in an elegant stance, he simply stands before us in the most natural, informal way, hands dug deep in his pockets, his bulk filling the canvas. A magic force seems to emanate from him. Typical of Goya's last years, the picture is painted in few colors, mostly a somber black, strikingly heightened by the bit of red vest showing, and yet, this restraint gives the effect of great richness and magnificence.

Satué was "Alcalde de Corte," one of the city councilors of Madrid until 1820, and subsequently a member of the Council for the Indies. He was born in 1765 and died in 1825. If the date of 1823 on the portrait is correct, which has sometimes been doubted, he would be shown at the age of fifty-eight. His robust appearance, fleshy face and thick, black hair, however, make him look younger. He has the air of a revolutionary and may well have had liberal leanings. It was in the house of his uncle, a clergyman, where Goya found refuge for three months when the liberal régime ended in 1823 and Ferdinand VII was restored to the throne.

20: THE MILKMAID OF BORDEAUX (about 1827), oil on canvas
29½" x 26¼", Prado, Madrid

This idyllic picture of a young maiden was painted late in Goya's life. Legend has it (incorrectly) that it was his last picture, and has thus given it an unjustly sentimental fame. Goya was never, not to his dying day, sentimental. Yet, the picture with its pensive and elegiac mood is unlike anything else in his work. Almost square and rather small, it gives an impression of monumentality. Placed oddly low and heavily into the bottom part of the canvas, the figure has a sculptural quality of massive volume. When Greuze painted his celebrated version of the eighteenth century milkmaid over fifty years earlier, he showed a pretty girl in languid pose, holding a ladle as an attribute of her trade. Greuze's "Laitière," now in the Louvre in Paris, is sentimental in its sweetish mixture of barely disguised frivolity and dishonest moral implication. With Goya the simple, banal person of a milkmaid takes on much larger and timeless proportions. She appears as a sort of Demeter, the mythical earth goddess, or one of the Fates who decide man's destiny and life span. A mystery emanates from the painting that allows many interpretations and thoughts. Like many great painters in their last days, Goya painted only the essential, nothing superfluous, nothing incidental. He tells no story. Instead, he has distilled the truth about human nature, which he had expounded in most of his work, into a symbol of womanhood and life itself.

There is no milk pail, no background, no object to the girl's dreamy, tender gaze, only a wide, atmospheric sky. Her proletarian ugliness is translated into beauty through the graceful rhythm of softly curving forms and outlines, and through sparkling colors. The picture is nothing but a manifestation of deep human compassion and painterly genius. In layer over layer of the loaded brush, Goya mixes greens and blues into a shimmering and translucent paint texture. A mantle of light envelopes the whole figure. This wonderful luminosity heralds the future art of Impressionism and makes the milkmaid ancestress to the women painted later by Corot and Renoir.